The Wonder
of It All

Revealed through
Poetry and Art

VALERIE J. BORGAL

WestBow Press books may be ordered through booksellers or by contacting:

WestBow Press
A Division of Thomas Nelson & Zondervan
1663 Liberty Drive
Bloomington, IN 47403
www.westbowpress.com
844-714-3454

Because of the dynamic nature of the Internet, any web addresses or links contained in this book may have changed since publication and may no longer be valid. The views expressed in this work are solely those of the author and do not necessarily reflect the views of the publisher, and the publisher hereby disclaims any responsibility for them.

Any people depicted in stock imagery provided by Getty Images are models, and such images are being used for illustrative purposes only.
Certain stock imagery © Getty Images.

Scripture quotations are taken from the New King James Version®. Copyright © 1982 by Thomas Nelson. Used by permission. All rights reserved.

Interior Image Credit: Valerie J. Borgal

ISBN: 978-1-6642-6154-9 (sc)
ISBN: 978-1-6642-6155-6 (e)

Library of Congress Control Number: 2022905364

Print information available on the last page.

WestBow Press rev. date: 07/28/2022

WESTBOW
PRESS®
A DIVISION OF THOMAS NELSON
& ZONDERVAN

Dedication

The Wonder of It All is dedicated to all the teachers in my life who
taught me and encouraged me to use my gifts and talents.

Most of all, I dedicate this work to the glory of God, who gives me ideas and comes
along side me to help me create and write. I am amazed by His leading, His wisdom,
and His love that He gives day in and day out. Jesus is my life. He shows me the way,
shares His truth, opens my mind to understand, and my heart to apply it.

Acknowledgments

Thank you to Linda Kapeckas for editing the manuscript, giving your time, and experience to help The **Wonder of It All** come to fruition.

Thank you to Karen Diaco and Sonja Schmidt. You read through the poetry and gave great critiques, ideas, and suggestions to improve the read in the middle of your busy lives.

Thank you to my husband, Tom Borgal, who sat alone in the evenings, while I worked on the computer. Thank you for your edits, suggestions, and your encouragement.

Thank you to all who have prayed for me during the process: my family, Bible Study Ladies, Church family, and those in the Matt Tommey's Created to Thrive mentoring group.

God guided me through the whole process and kept me at peace. To Him be the glory: He is my Lord, Savior, Guide, Wisdom, always present, leading the way I should go. We co-created together in paintings and poetry writing. Thank You, Lord! It is exciting to work with You!

Introduction

Over my life time, I have written numerous poems and painted many works of art. I wrote these poems in <u>The Wonder of It All</u> between 1994 and 2022 and created the artwork between 2000 and 2022. Over the past two years, I have culled through my poetry to share the best with you. Along with the poems I have brought in my artwork to compliment each poem: giving you, the reader, a little more to ponder by using the eyes to stir the imagination as you read the words. You will read poems about nature, critters in my life, people I love, places I have ventured and about my faith.

I pray you will be blessed as you read, chuckle, and even laugh out loud, maybe shedding a tear or two, think and ponder, and feel a tug on your heart from the Lord.

Valerie J. Borgal

Contents

Faith

Author's Testimony

My Palette

Watercolor
Valerie J. Borgal

An Artist's Witness

All of my talents are a gift from God,
given to me to honor my Lord.
But long ago, my heart was far from Him,
lost in my sin, but life did not look too grim.
Deep down inside, I was lying to myself.
The answers I needed were in my Bible on the shelf.
God moved in my heart and revealed Himself to me.
Reading the Gospel of John, I began to see.
God created me and had a plan for my life-
to make me His child, ending sin and strife.
Believing in Jesus that on the cross He did die,
to save me from my sins, I know because God can't lie.
From that day until now, Jesus has been my Savior and Friend.
He forgives me, loves me, even after this life comes to an end.
I look forward to the day when His face I will see
when I arrive in heaven to live with Him for eternity.
God made you. He loves you. You are precious to Him, too.
He has a plan for your life for you to do.
Without Jesus as Savior, you are dead in your sin.
Heaven's Gates are closed; you will not get in.
God sent His Son to die for you and me.
Believe Him and receive eternal life; you will see.
The Bible is God's Word. Trust what He says today,
to bring peace to your life and let Him show you His way.
God will bless you as you grow to become like His Son,
receiving His blessings and the victory He has already won!
I am grateful for the gifts and talents He has given to me;
to God be all praise, thanksgiving, and majesty!

Valerie J. Borgal
1999

But thanks be to God, who gives us the victory through our Lord Jesus Christ.
1Cor. 15:57
NKJV

Nature

Furry Backyard Clown

I see you, Mr. Squirrel, my furry backyard clown.
You jump and twist and flip in the air, and never fall down.
Chasing your buddies through the trees with speeds I wouldn't dare.
You're unaware of danger or you just don't seem to care.

Playing follow the leader, chasing, jumping, flying through space.
Made it! You didn't come falling down, landing on your face.
Frisky little fellow, you run through your courses with ease,
as you travel or' the "highways" through the gentle breeze.

You are on guard for predators, who might make you their meal.
Waiting, perched high on a limb, your tail you wave and reel.
Chattering, yelling, and crying out! Everyone's put on guard.
Waiting for the enemy to move on, I know that's very hard.

If you can wait it out, patience will give its reward.
After a while, the menace moves away growing very bored.
You're off again as you scamper and wrestle with a friend.
A blessing from our Creator, you are, that seems to never end.

As long as you don't get inside, you nosy little critter,
You eat the screens and gnaw the wood; my heart turns very bitter.
No! No! No, you don't! Little squirrels belong outside!
You stay right where you're meant to be, so you don't end up fried.

And stay out of my bird feeder, pigging out on all my seed.
It's intended for my feathered friends that you are keeping treed.
You're an amiable clown, as long as you keep your place.
Eating acorns in a tree or running a speedy race.

Jumping in and out of bushes, and flipping all around,
leaping quickly onto tree trunks and then back to the ground.
Or flattening yourself out on my deck to bask in the sun,
only to jump up, give a scratch, and quickly turn and run.

You make me laugh out loud as I watch your crazy antics.
You are the best entertainment, better than TV flicks.
Just stay out of trouble and I'll love having you around.
You're a frisky little fellow, my furry backyard clown.

By Valerie J. Borgal
3\3\2000

Furry Backyard Clown

Pen and Ink stippling
by Valerie J.Borgal

Frosty

Watercolor/pen & ink
Valerie J. Borgal

The Frosty Catcher

Lying on the deck one sunny day;
I noticed an intruder coming our way.
The geese are back with their scrawny litter,
pooping on our lawn, such a persistent critter.

I sound the alarm and run to the rescue,
over the lawn across morning dew.
Do not worry, Mom, everything is under control!
I'll get those feathery beasts on my Frosty Patrol.

Into the water, I leap with a bound;
off for the chase, following that horrible honking sound:
Barking, and yapping, and telling them off;
I'll catch you and turn you into Goose Stroganoff!

Oh, no, here comes Mom to catch me and haul me home,
in her Frosty Catcher with oars sounding like a metronome.
I must get those geese before she gets me.
"I can do it, Mom! You will see!"

I swim faster; I'm starting to gain
on the big feathery feisty birdbrain.
UGH!
Oh, Mom, you spoiled my attack, you saboteur!
I was going in for the kill for your soup du jour.

Look! They are getting away,
only to return another day.
I might as well give a shake before I catch a chill.
Do not yell! Okay! Okay! I'll sit and be still.

May I kiss you, my chauffeur,
as you row me home in my Frosty Catcher?
No? Okay, I will just sit here and rest.
I love you, Mom! You are the best!

Valerie J. Borgal
The Frosty Catcher was written for Frosty to my Mom for her birthday.
2000

Frosty Catcher

Watercolor/pen & ink
Valerie J. Borgal

Frosty was a white Bichon Frise, my mother's constant companion for many years. He was spoiled, and he loved it. He was always trying to get her attention: ready to play, get petted, or fed, or go out and do his duty. His favorite dessert was a spoonful of ice cream. If he did not eat his dinner; he would go lay down. If he ate his dinner, he would sit by her chair and beg for his spoonful of ice cream. He would start with a low growl, then a loud growl. Next, came a little yip, which brought him to his feet, followed by a loud bark. My mom was hard-of-hearing, but I think she just pretended she couldn't hear him. When Frosty had her attention, she would ask him, "Do you want good ice cream?" He answered by licking his face. She would ask a second time, to be sure, and he would lick his face again. Only then would she get up and give him his spoonful, which he lapped up and was satisfied. Frosty was a goose, moose, squirrel, and heron chaser; he never caught one. Mom always worried that the geese would drown him when he swam after them. She would row after Frosty and bring him back home.

Bugs

Pen and Ink
Valerie J. Borgal

Bugs

God made all the bugs, every itsy bitsy one.
I sometimes wonder why 'cause some are not much fun.
They bite and sting and make me jump and itch and run.
I get bumps and scratch and scratch every itchy one.

But itchy bumpy lumps do fade away real quick.
I've learned to stay away from bugs that make me sick:
like fire ants, bees and beetles, and the little tick,
and yellow jackets trying to get my corn for a lick.

God didn't make a mistake when the cricket sings.
Bugs feed the birds, skunks, bats, and other furry things.
When I go outside to explore what this day brings,
I know that bugs will be among my biggest blessings!

Lying in the grass the flies buzz 'round my nose,
and soon a little ant is crawling up my toes.
I brush him off and watch to find out where he goes,
down into a hole in the ground where no one knows.

I like to see the butterfly that brightens up my way,
and grasshoppers who jump, and jump so far away,
and when I see the ladybugs so bright I say,
"Thank you, God, for making bugs to watch this summer day!"

Valerie J. Borgal
1996

Written to the honor and glory of God, our wonderful Creator,
and for my K-4 class at Fellowship Christian Academy in Methuen, MA
to sing during the Bug Parade through all the classrooms.

And God made the beast of the earth according to its kind, cattle according to its kind,
and everything that creeps on the earth according to its kind. And God saw that it was good.
Gen. 1:24-25
NKJV

Leaf Pile

Watercolor
Valerie J. Borgal

Late Autumn Conversation

Look! There! Oh, how bright!
The moon, hanging in the dark blue sky, round and white!
God's flashlight is shining on us tonight,
while dark wispy clouds rush by in rapid flight.

We name the other planets' moons that we identify,
But we call our moon – Moon. I wonder why?
God named it Moon when He placed it in the sky.
Why change what He said is good? I would not try.

The air is warm, as the balmy winds blow;
Rains coming tonight, don't you know?
Such a tease, this autumn warmth with this shining glow.
We know it will not be long; we will be blanketed in snow.

Some rusty oak leaves are hanging on, resisting
their flight through the air to another year of recycling.
New England maples lost their yellow and orange dressing.
It was drab this autumn with the bright reds missing.

Lots of rain and warm weather may be the reason.
The colors were not as bright as last season.
Guess we cannot expect God to paint glorious colors again and again.
We have only had one hard frost this fall; we certainly haven't been freezin'!

Tonight we will accept this warm blessing God has sent,
with the silhouettes of undressed trees against the deep blue tent.
For this is New England! And we know her bent.
But, tonight, we will enjoy this reprieve, if only for a moment.

Valerie J. Borgal
2005

"While the earth remains, Seedtime and harvest, Cold and heat, Winter and summer,
And day and night Shall not cease."
Gen. 8:22
NKJV

The Wonders In My Backyard

Lord, You gave me two new birds in my backyard today.
As I see each, I am in awe of Your creative display.
You give me so much joy in these treasures; you are so kind.
Thank You for the beauty and variety I find.

Flying near they land on branches, such a marvelous sight,
in the early morning sun their colors glow so bright;
thank You for the morning chirps, caws, and each trill.
The wonder of it all gives my heart a thrill!

You are so faithful, Lord, to bring back each season;
to show You keep Your promises and give us a reason,
to believe You are the Mighty Creator, God of all the ages,
from eternity past, written by Your sages.

On the fifth day of creation, You put the birds in flight.
You must have sung and jumped for joy at the wondrous sight.
All around the world, people enjoy the beauty of Your creations.
They shout for joy and sing aloud with hearty jubilations.

A gray tuxedoed Junco appears and a Chickadee in his black cap.
Woodpeckers are wearing their checks as their beaks for insects tap.
Timid cooing Mourning Doves, cooing a sound so smooth and sweet,
peck, peck, pecking at the ground for ants, a tasty treat.

American crows so big and black, grasping tree tops with huge claws,
guarding the feeding ground, these soldiers shout warnings with noisy caws!
Bold Blue Jays, brazen bullies, so beautiful in cobalt blue, black, and white;
they love eating cheese crackers until startled and quickly take flight.

There is that silly little bird, the Nuthatch, what a clown!
He walks on the sides of trees upside-down.
The Tufted Titmouse quickly flits about in pointed crest;
I wonder where he goes to build his simple little nest.

The iridescent Grackles and Cowbirds gather around.
Spring is here, and my heart sings to see them on the ground.
A Northern Flicker came to my feeder and stayed a while.
Today, a Carolina Wren stopped by with tail sticking up in style.

Flying into the swamp, the Mallards have come back.
They greet me each morning with their hearty, "Quack-quack!"
From bushes, I hear chatter and notice fluttering wings.
Sparrows congregate to discuss important things.

The Mocking Bird, true to his name, sings a little ditty.
A Cardinal appears in his red suit with black ascot so pretty.
The neighbor's cat crouches nearby for a tasty treat to stalk.
I see the lightning, striking, swoop of the Red-tailed Hawk.

Lord, I sit in awe of all the drama You put in my backyard.
I see Your handiwork, for You it was not hard.
With Your voice, Your powerful Word, You spoke it into being.
Thank You for the wonders in my backyard I am seeing.

Valerie J. Borgal
2000

This poem was written to the honor and glory of God, who created all these wonderful feathered friends; and dedicated to my Mom, Jeanne Riley Camber Conley. She taught me to appreciate and recognize these backyard critters. Many thanks to our friendly Birder, Hugh Wiberg, from Wilmington, MA: for challenging me to move in closer and know them individually.

Backyard Visitor

Watercolor
Valerie J. Borgal

For by Him all things were created that are in heaven and that are on earth, visible and invisible, whether thrones or dominions or principalities or powers. All things were created through Him and for Him.
Col. 1:16
NKJV

Game of Tag

Pen & Ink
Valerie J. Borgal

Game of Tag

The sun's out bright, and the critters do play.
Lying in their nest is not their way.
Nine squirrels tearing through the backyard,
chasing across the ground frozen so hard.
Scurrying up trees and out over branches:
flying through the air, taking risky chances.
Landing and grasping onto a nearby tree;
it's a game of tag and living carefree.

Rounding the trunk, one after another:
father, mother, sisters, and brothers.
After an hour of racing and playing around;
all slow down and begin searching the ground
for nibbles and treats, looking here and there.
One burrows in leaves and comes up with air.
Jumping up on the woodpile for a rest,
looking around with an eye on the pest.

Little rascal wants to play with someone.
He runs straight at another, wanting some fun.
Taunting and teasing, then jumping away,
waiting to see if his brother will play.
But brother sits, not taking the bait.
Off the rascal goes because he can't wait.
Tagging another, and the game is on,
playing tag freely across the frozen lawn!

Valerie J. Borgal
2021

12

What am I?

There are big ones and small ones found on your face,
on your arms, and back, and most any old place.
The ones on your face, because they are visible,
make many people very miserable.
They cause some folks to heckle
all because of me; I am a freckle!

Valerie J. Borgal
2021

Son Shine

Graphite
Valerie J. Borgal

I will praise You, for I am fearfully and wonderfully made; Marvelous are Your works, And that my soul knows very well. My frame was not hidden from You, When I was made in secret, And skillfully wrought in the lowest parts of the earth. Your eyes saw my substance, being yet unformed. And in Your book they all were written, The days fashioned for me, When as yet there were none of them.

Psalm 139:14- 16
NKJV

Blueberries

Watercolor
Valerie J. Borgal

A Bountiful Blueberry Day

We were off to New Hampshire under an overcast sky
to go blueberry picking went Evelyn and I.
With a bucket in hand, "You will need a bigger one!" she said,
as I walked into a field covered with netting above my head.

There were rows of high bush blueberries as far as we could see.
We were assigned our bushes; we got three.
God's bountiful blessings spread over the land.
Clusters of blue, round balls rolled into my hand.

With buckets three-quarters full, we needed new employment.
We were given two new bushes for our picking enjoyment.
Stripping them bare with buckets filled to the top;
we decided that it was time to stop.

We lined up to pay for our blueberry bounty;
Then, we were off to the old homestead in Rockingham county.
As we hiked over the old carriage trails,
Evelyn told some of the family tales.

There were places she remembered picking as a child
with blueberries, raspberries, and blackberries growing wild.
Now the pines grew tall; no berries in sight.
That was okay; our buckets were full to our delight.

Then we were off to meet her friend, Gladys,
with Larkspurs and Black-Eyed Susans gracing a home so modest.
A feisty little woman 92 years young
welcomed us into her kitchen warmed by the sun.

Next, off to the cemetery to see Ma and Pa's gravestone.
We spruced up the flowers and pulled weeds over-grown.
Now the stone could be seen, and names read,
as we showed our respect to those who were dead.

But one more stop we just had to make.
It was a ride around Searles Castles for an unusual take.
Then homeward bound chatting all the way,
bringing an end to a wonder-filled, memorable day.

Valerie J. Borgal
9/29/2000

I wrote this poem for Evelyn McCarthy, a good friend to my Mom and me.

Then God said, "Let the earth bring forth grass, the herb that yields seed, and the fruit tree that yields fruit according to its kind, whose seed is in itself, on the earth"; and it was so. And the earth brought forth grass, the herb that yields seed according to its kind, and the tree that yields fruit, whose seed is in itself according to its kind. And God saw that it was good. So the evening and the morning were the third day.

Gen 1:11-13
NKJV

The Cottage

Watercolor/Pen & Ink
Valerie J. Borgal

At The Cottage

The Monhegan Island flavor was all around.
Gulls call in the distance while the surfs pound
granite rocks: the foundation which holds up the isle
and the bright fluorescent orange buoy bobs beside a boat in style.
The lighthouse atop the hill with the museum sparkling bright
looks down on the village and out onto Manana's green rocky sight.
Quiet and quaint, but rustic and worn,
with deep shadows of pines cast across the lawn.
The laundry dances in the breezy air;
just hanging around without one care.
Geraniums in the window box: a colorful sight,
graces the eyes of the beholder to their delight.
The cottage door, always open, welcomes a friend;
the sun sets in splendorous colors at the day's end.
It makes the heart sing and gives the spirit a lift.
God had blessed the day with His beauty; a wonderful gift.

Valerie J. Borgal
8/20/2002

Monhegan Island is a destination for an adventure for a day trip or an overnight stay. Seventeen miles of trails on an island 1 3/4 miles long and 1/2 mile wide and sits 10 miles off the coast of Maine, offers inspiring sights. Birding is very popular, and of course, artists have spent many days painting on Monhegan. There is no lack of subject matter. It seems like everywhere you look, something is beckoning for your attention. There are quaint cottages, rustic and weathered boathouses, buoy mounds and lobster pots piled high, boats, magnificent flower gardens add to the sights and flavor of the island, windblown pines, a lighthouse, a one-room schoolhouse, a church, and a quaint library. The rocky shores and high cliffs on the east side give a breathtaking view of the vast Atlantic. There is a shipwreck on the southeastern shore: a reminder of the strength of the surf, and a warning for all, to be careful on the rocks.

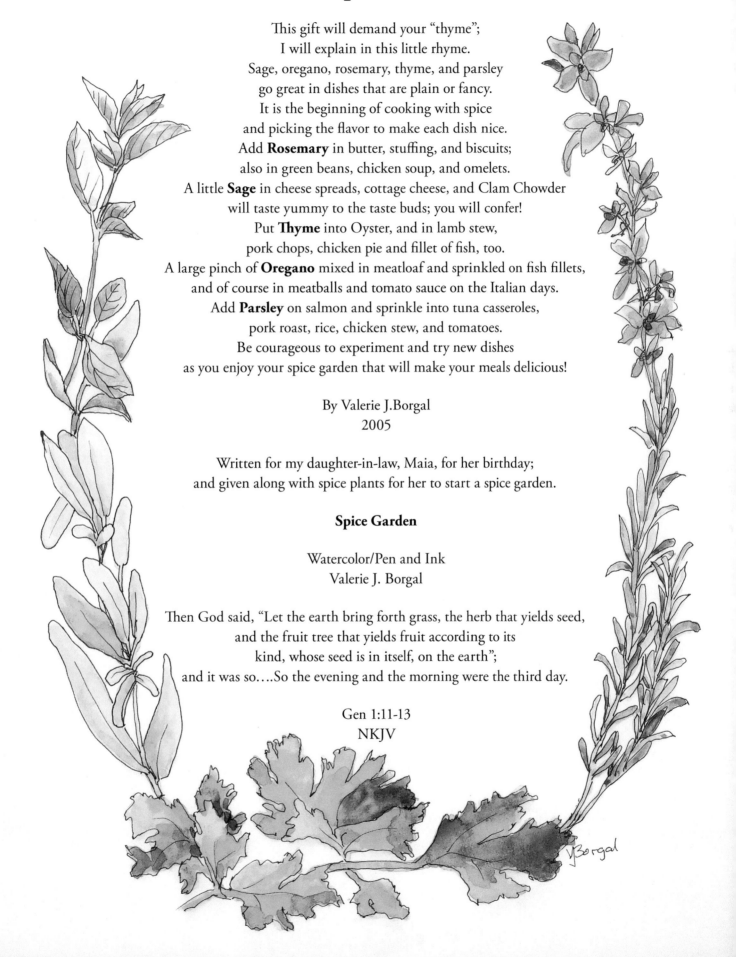

The Spice Garden

This gift will demand your "thyme";
I will explain in this little rhyme.
Sage, oregano, rosemary, thyme, and parsley
go great in dishes that are plain or fancy.
It is the beginning of cooking with spice
and picking the flavor to make each dish nice.
Add **Rosemary** in butter, stuffing, and biscuits;
also in green beans, chicken soup, and omelets.
A little **Sage** in cheese spreads, cottage cheese, and Clam Chowder
will taste yummy to the taste buds; you will confer!
Put **Thyme** into Oyster, and in lamb stew,
pork chops, chicken pie and fillet of fish, too.
A large pinch of **Oregano** mixed in meatloaf and sprinkled on fish fillets,
and of course in meatballs and tomato sauce on the Italian days.
Add **Parsley** on salmon and sprinkle into tuna casseroles,
pork roast, rice, chicken stew, and tomatoes.
Be courageous to experiment and try new dishes
as you enjoy your spice garden that will make your meals delicious!

By Valerie J.Borgal
2005

Written for my daughter-in-law, Maia, for her birthday;
and given along with spice plants for her to start a spice garden.

Spice Garden

Watercolor/Pen and Ink
Valerie J. Borgal

Then God said, "Let the earth bring forth grass, the herb that yields seed,
and the fruit tree that yields fruit according to its
kind, whose seed is in itself, on the earth";
and it was so….So the evening and the morning were the third day.

Gen 1:11-13
NKJV

Junco No Doubt

There you are in your coat of white and gray,
searching here and there on this cloudy day,
pecking, turning, head bobbing up and down
for a morsel to eat from off the ground.
You stay for a while, hopping about;
your Creator feeds you. You don't doubt.

But for me, oh no, I doubt.
Off in my willfulness I strike out.
I rack my brain and go no place.
Then I remembered God's amazing grace.
With Him to do life, He invited me to do.
It's easy. It's light: all provided, too.

Yes, Jesus, Your way proves to be the best.
In it, much is accomplished, and I am blest.
God, guide and empower me in all I do.
You are so faithful; I praise and worship You.
Help me to trust Your Holy Spirit to lead,
as I read Your word; my spirit You feed.

I watch this Junco searching for food;
You provided for him and his little brood.
With his seed, he flies to the old oak tree,
I remember, You always care for me.
A great teacher, little Junco, in a coat of white and gray
No doubting, but trusting our Creator God is the best way.

Valerie J. Borgal
2021

Look at the birds of the air, for they neither sow nor reap nor gather into barns;
yet your heavenly Father feeds them. Are you not of more value than they?
Matt.6:26
NJKV

Junco

Watercolor
Valerie J. Borgal

SKUNKS

S tinky, smelly, phew!
K eep your stink with you!
U p into my nose, your odors go.
N ever a stench goes away so slow:
K eeping in the air a putrid residue.
S tinky, smelly, phew!

Valerie J. Borgal
2008

I wrote this poem after I was rudely awakened in the middle of the night by the gross smell of a skunk.

Stinky

Scratchboard
Valerie J. Borgal
2018

Then God saw everything that He had made, and indeed it was very good.
So the evening and the morning were the sixth day.
Gen. 1:3
NKJV

Tufted Titmouse

Tufted Titmouse, my little friend,
your flights to my feeder never end.
Dressed in your blue-gray feathered suit
with your tufted cap; you sure look cute.
Taking one sunflower seed is your gig,
then to the forsythia, you land on a twig.
Tapping the seed between your feet,
breaking it open for your tasty treat.
Any time of the day, you are welcome to come.
I'll be looking for you, my tufted chum.

Valerie J. Borgal

Spring Awakening

Watercolor / pen & ink
Valerie J. Borgal

Then God said, …, and let birds fly above the earth across the face of the firmament of the heavens."

Gen. 1:20
NKJV

People and Places

Playing in the Cellar

Playing in the cellar
pipes and rafters above,
cement floor under my feet,
the coolness I love.

I scoot under the table.
It's a hiding place for me,
like a bear's dark cave.
I'm as happy as can be.

No one can see me.
But I can see you.
I suddenly jump out
with a great big, "Boo!"

I can use my imagination
to think of things to play,
while playing in the cellar
on a hot summer's day.

Valerie J. Borgal
4/2021

Playing in the Cellar

Watercolor
Valerie J. Borgal

Child Of God

C hrist Jesus is your Good Shepherd,
H elping His sheep walk heavenward.
I sn't He wonderful this Prince of Peace,
L oving you with love that will never cease,
D ying for you on Calvary's Cross,

O ffering His blood to wash away sin's dross,
F orgiven and blessed by His marvelous grace,

G od has taken away all your disgrace.
O nly in Jesus are you forever free,
D epending on Him into eternity.

Valerie J. Borgal
1999

This poem was written for children who put their trust in Jesus for their salvation.

I'd Rather Be A Door Keeper

Watercolor
Valerie J. Borgal

The Pig-tailed Girl

It was a wonderful day in the backyard
as the sun was shining bright.
On the lawn, dark shadows played
against the dazzling sunlight.

Even better than the warmth of the sun
was the pig-tailed girl who warmed my heart,
as she stooped and petted me,
instead of doing her art.

Her kind hand smoothed down my fur
from my head down to my tail.
It felt so wonderful,
but her art I did derail.

I rubbed myself up against her
and purred to my heart's content,
while her brushes and paper waited
along with her pretty pigment.

I walked off into the tall leaves
of the daylilies now gone by,
and disappeared within the growth;
I don't know why.

Soon I reappeared
disguised as a floppy-green-eared rabbit,
sneaking out from my hiding place,
but she did not fall for it.

I noticed all my fur
she was trying to remove from her clothes.
She got it all off
knowing it affects her mother's nose.

I enjoyed a wonderful day
as I stretched with a great big yawn.
The pig-tailed girl went back to her painting,
while I relaxed in the sun on the lawn.

Valerie J. Borgal
1999

I dedicate this poem to my wonderfully talented art student, the pig-tailed girl, Katie Wuthrich.

Floppy Green Eared Rabbit?

Watercolor
Valerie J. Borgal

His Hats

Donning his hat on that sunny day,
off to Plymouth, Massachusetts, we went to play.
A Mayflower sailor asked, "Is that beaver pelt?"
"No." He answered, "It's just felt."

Felt dyed a deep mauve, not grape;
pressed and put into just the right shape.
A thin brown band was added for trim,
with three dark holes looking over the brim.

Then there is his hat of tan pigskin,
that keeps the sun from shining in.
It's covered with pores where a sow's hair once grew;
now it protects his head where his hairs once grew, too!

Throughout the years, hats have come and gone.
A white pug cap worn to picnics on the lawn,
and an olive safari hat with netting in the crown:
right brim snapped up, and the other side left down.

Making paths with the snow-blower he steers
with a stocking cap pulled down over his ears.
In awhile, his ears would be showing,
exposed to the cold and the bitter wind's blowing.

Then out to Pemaquid Light to watch bursting surf
rolling over sun-struck granite as we sat on the turf.
He dons his hat with a face a bit silly:
no, not him, his smiling tan Tilley.

Ah! Another we see atop of a head.
A smile and a nod, but nothing said.
Two hatters acknowledge their family line;
they are looking good, just fine!

So many hats over the years he has worn;
it is amazing since he donned them with muttering scorn.
Much protection is needed,
learned from hard lessons; he has finally heeded.

Vanity has lost her fight and receives no glory.
Common sense has won, so ends this story.
For those who still struggle with vanities plight;
put on the hat of common sense and win the fight.

Valerie J. Borgal
2001

The Smiling Hat

Watercolor
Valerie J. Borgal

"Vanity of vanities," says the Preacher, "All is vanity."
Ecc. 12:8
NKJV

Jeanne's Life at the Silver Gull

Jeanne keeps right on going.
On her John Deere, she's out mowing,
a whack by a branch and a brand new lump,
picking up twigs and trips to the dump.

Growing her flowers and pruning her shrubs:
watering her garden and squishing potato bugs.
Feeding the birds, Tom turkey, and brood,
holidays with family and friends, and lots of good food.

She must do the Jumble every day,
and to Evelyn, the answer she does relay.
Doing crossword puzzles and reading her books,
there's crypt-o-quip, and giving the geese dirty looks.

"Keep moving!" is the order of the day.
Goose poop on her lawn, no way!
And when Frosty decides to be a goose chaser
Jeanne rows after him in her Frosty Catcher.

Racing Connor in her rowboat,
she thinks she won as she will gloat.
The big race is on, so weighty it's clear,
with Jack, her great-grandson, on his little John Deere.

She grows plants and earns a high score,
a red orchid cactus with seventy-five flowers or more.
There are blueberries to sort and freeze,
along with carrots, beans, and peas.

A Pileated Woodpecker pair appeared one day.
They landed in the Choke Cherry trees for a stay.
Jeanne loves her birds: knows each chirp and call,
and keeps the feeder filled for one and all.

There is more mowing of her pristine lawn,
plus watering, weeding, and waiting for corn.
Oh, and don't forget in the winter she shovels the snow;
and with a snow-blower, the snow she does blow.

To family and friends, she is a great hostess
and her food is amazingly delicious.
At the Silver Gull Country Club life is first-rate.
Now it's Jeanne's life we celebrate!

Valerie J. Borgal
2012

Jeanne and Frosty

Watercolor
Valerie J. Borgal

Surely goodness and mercy shall follow me All the days of my life;
And I will dwell in the house of the LORD Forever.
Psalm 23:6
NKJV

A Message in a Bottle

A message in a bottle of cobalt blue glass.

H oping today, you do not need to mow the grass,
A s narcissus bloom around your yard.
P retty as a picture; enjoying them will not be hard.
P ut yourself in a chair and relax with a glass of iced tea.
Y ou deserve a break; it is plain to see.

M y one and only Mom is a better mom than all of them.
O n Mother's day, I send you this poem,
T o celebrate you on this day,
H elper, friend, guiding our way,
E ver planting, mowing, crossword puzzling,
R eading, rowing, birding, or scrabbling.
S o, to you, I give a cheer!

D ialing the phone, you are always near
A lways ready to share with another,
Y ou are my one and only, especially loved MOTHER!

Valerie J. Borgal

This poem was a gift to my Mom on Mother's Day 2006, shipped to her in a cobalt blue glass bottle, which she enjoyed collecting.

They shall still bear fruit in old age; They shall be fresh and flourishing,
Psalm 92:14
NKJV

Message in a Bottle

Watercolor
Valerie J. Borgal

2018

"HONOR YOUR FATHER AND MOTHER,"
which is the first commandment with promise:
Eph. 6:2
NKJV

Ears a' Ringing

Watercolor
Valerie J. Borgal

Ears a' Ringing

Ears a' ringing,
Ding-a-ling-ing,
Jingle belling,
Oh, the swelling,
Hissing, clicking,
Snapping, crackling,
Sounds a' reveling,
Steam pipes whistling,
Overwhelming,
Steam pipes whistling,
Sounds a' reveling,
Snapping, crackling,
Hissing, clicking,
Oh, the swelling,
Jingle belling,
Ding-a-ling-ing,
Ears a' ringing!

Valerie J. Borgal
2010

This poem is dedicated to my ear ringing family members.

And He said to me, "My grace is sufficient for you, for My strength is made perfect in weakness."
Therefore most gladly I will rather boast in my infirmities, that the power of Christ may rest upon me.
2 Cor. 12:9 NKJV

The Mug Shot

Holding a pitcher of milk, he called to me.
I turned and wondered what this could be.
Standing posing, he asked, "How about a mug shot?"
And a pitcher of milk and his mug were what he got.

As I pulled my camera from where it is hidden,
he began to protest, "Oh, No!! I was kiddin'!"
"You asked for it," I said, "and I came equipped.
A mug shot you shall have, just as you quipped."

Trapped by his joke; it was not an awful disgrace,
as he posed good-natured with a smile on his face.
With the pitcher and his mug, not so poker,
he's now on record as the NEBC Joker.

Valerie Borgal
2/11/2002

This poem was written and dedicated to Doug Lobley, the NEBC Joker. NEBC (New England Bible Church, Andover, MA) is where we attend church. Doug always had a joke to share with anyone who would listen. This time he got caught in his joke. Doug has since gone home to be with Jesus. I know he is still telling his jokes and giving Jesus a chuckle.

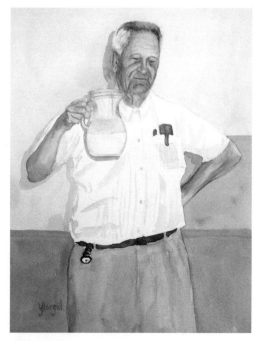

The Joker

Watercolor
Valerie J. Borgal

Will You Still Love Me When I Make a Mess

Watercolor
Valerie J. Borgal

The LORD has appeared of old to me, saying:
"Yes, I have loved you with an everlasting love;
Therefore with lovingkindness, I have drawn you.

Jer. 31:3
NKJV

Will You Still Love Me?

A new adventure is waiting each day,
new places to explore, and new things to play.
I may dump all my food onto the floor,
or even hurl it at the door,
to hear its splats, or plops, or pings!
I am learning about gravity and flying things!
I do not want to cause you distress.
Will you still love me when I make a mess?

My world is so big; there is so much to explore.
Please come and join me down here on the floor.
There are many textures to touch, sounds to hear, colors to view,
flavors to taste, scents to smell, especially of you.
You smell so good, and you are soft to touch.
When I'm in your arms, I love you so much.
I feel secure and safe in your warm caress;
but I wonder, will you still love me when I make a mess?

Please try not to squelch all my How comes? and Whys?;
when I have asked enough questions to reach up to the skies.
Be patient with my curiosity,
because our God has built that into me.
He wants me to learn and discover the truth:
about Him, about me, and about my loose tooth.
Discipline me when I'm willful; I will not love you less.
But, please, continue to love me when I make a mess.

Valerie J. Borgal
1994

Those Wonderful Hugs

Those hugs that you get
when you come in or leave.
They surround you with more love
than you could ever believe.
Some are gentle, some strong,
some quick, and some long.
Some are low, some are high,
and some meet you eye to eye.
But no matter which kind of hug you get,
the same message comes through that you never forget.
It says, "I love you, with no strings attached."
And that's a message not easily matched.

Valerie Borgal
1997

Sweet Friendship

Watercolor/Pen & Ink
Valerie J. Borgal

Be kindly affectionate to one another with brotherly love, in honor giving preference to one another;
Rom 12:10
NKJV

Bryan's Apple

Watercolor
Valerie J. Borgal

Smolak Farm

We're riding down to Smolak's.
It is an apple farm.
Riding the hay wagon
around the great big barn.
Picking apples from the trees
or pumpkins from the ground.
To the barn for cider
and donuts, good and round.
Do, do, do, do, do, do, do, do,
DO - NUTS!

Valerie J. Borgal
1994

Smolak Farm in North Andover, MA, is a wonderful experience for my K-4 class
to have a day of apple picking, hayride, animal petting and feeding, pumpkin
picking, munching on apple cider donuts, and drinking apple cider.

then I will give you rain in its season, the land shall yield its produce,
and the trees of the field shall yield their fruit.
Lev. 26:4
NKJV

Our Down Maine Trip

We packed our bags and were on our way;
off to Maine went Mina and I one day.
Talking and enjoying each new site,
looking forward to seeing the Nubble Light.

Chowda' for lunch, nothing else would do
to complement the rugged coastal view.
Our destination, the little town of Bremen,
where Frosty and Mom were awaitin'.

Greetings and dinner and a good night's rest;
down Maine cooking is always the best.
The morning excursion brought us to Round Pond,
with the sun sparkling on the ocean with islands beyond.

On into New Harbor with a quaint little cove,
then down the long finger of the coast we drove.
Arriving at Pemaquid Lighthouse at last,
we settled in our chairs and viewed the ocean so vast.

It was a beautiful day, an invigorating sight,
reminding us of Jesus our light.
With waves crashing and blue skies above
we couldn't help but sense our God's love.

Valerie J. Borgal
2001

I wrote this poem in memory of my down Maine trip with a sweet friend
and sister in the Lord, Mina Valentine, for her 90th birthday.

Pemaquid Beauties

Watercolor
Valerie J. Borgal

Then Jesus spoke to them again, saying, "I am the light of the world.
He who follows Me shall not walk in darkness, but have the light of life.

John 8:12
NKJV

Path to the River

Watercolor
Valerie J. Borgal

Maudslay Park

Out for a walk in Maudslay Park went Wilma, Vicky, and I.
It was a brisk day with the sun shining through a wispy, cloudy sky.
Rhododendron, twenty feet tall in a gentle breeze, did sway.
As God displayed his handiwork, we marveled along the way.
We gazed and stood in awe of the beauty we could see.
Then Vicky led us through poison ivy to the dismay of Wilma and me.
We talked and shared important things that God's doing in our lives.
We shared God's Word that encourages, blesses and edifies.
Sitting on a rock watching the Merrimac River as it passes by,
Having sweet fellowship in Maudsley's Park were Wilma, Vicky, and I.

Valerie J. Borgal
9/26/2000

But if we walk in the light as He is in the light,
we have fellowship with one another,
and the blood of Jesus Christ His Son cleanses us from all sin.
1John 1:7
NKJV

Fishing in the rain
Holding rod and umbrella
At the river's edge.

Fishing in the Rain

Watercolor
Valerie J. Borgal

Sing to the LORD with thanksgiving; Sing praises on the harp to our God,
Who covers the heavens with clouds,
Who prepares rain for the earth,
Who makes grass to grow on the mountains.

Psalm 147:7-8
NKJV

Back Cove

Watercolor
Valerie J. Borgal

Unexpected Blessings

Down Maine to celebrate Mom's birthday number seventy-eight
and to the Jicha's for a home-cooked meal we ate.
With John in the dishpan after we all did sup,
the conversation led to the Allen Island Sheep Round-up.

I got an invitation to come aboard Dot II;
found me driving into the Back Cove with a picture-postcard view.
Stowed and motoring under the overcast sky on the sea,
it was an unexpected blessing for me.

The sea was as calm as desert sand,
passing by the big buoy; and toward Eastern Egg Island.
No Puffins seen, but a seal pops up for a peek.
Off in the distance, we see Camden Mountain Peak.

Docking on Allen Island and joining the volunteer group:
we wondered, "Where are the sheep? What's the scoop?"
We waited around; "What now? What's happening?
"Don't move, be quiet," came the orders, "They are up at the opening."

Sheep were following the shepherd; as she shook a container of grain,
walking down a path to the pen over rugged terrain.
"Oh, no!" They stop and look at us, "Will they keep going?"
Soon they look to the shepherd and to their pen they are moving.

As the last one enters the pen, there's a cheer from the crowd!
However, "There are more to be found." Our leader calls out loud.
Off to the woods, three groups of runners go searching sheep out.
Down the road forms a human fence, listening for the shout.

They move up the road, keeping the sheep near the water.
No need to fear, little sheep; this isn't a slaughter.
It's only to shear off your wool and give you a check-up
and send you off 'til next October's round-up.

These sheep try to avoid what is best;
With their shepherd, they choose to test.
We are not much different when it comes to making a choice.
We sometimes don't listen to our Shepherd's voice.

Black Sheep

Watercolor
Valerie J. Borgal

Some sheep had eluded the scouts and remained in the woods.
Their wool would not become the shearer's dry goods.
After chasing the black lamb, I felt winded and ram shackled;
that breakaway, surefooted, black, blur was soon tackled.

Coffee and muffins satisfied the volunteers while dinner was awaiting.
In the barn, boys and girls were joyfully swinging.
Andrew, Betsy, Jamie, and Nicholas by boat did arrive;
they joined the crowd with thankful handshakes for the sheep drive.

Our appetites satisfied with delicious Maine victuals galore,
we wave our good-byes and head down over the rocky shore.
Aboard Dot II, the sea and sky before us did stretch.
I contemplated God's far vaster love for this wretch.

Remembering my shepherd; who sought after me,
never realized how wonderful my life would be.
As we headed to the cove over the wavy wind-blown sea,
I was thankful for the unexpected blessings God had poured upon me.

Valerie J. Borgal
2000

Andrew

Watercolor
Valerie J. Borgal

All we like sheep have gone astray; we have turned everyone to his own way;
and the Lord hath laid on him the iniquity of us all.
Isaiah 53:6
NKJV

Faith

The Cana Cross

Watercolor
Valerie J. Borgal

Wedding Prayer

Jesus, dear Savior,
please bless these two lovers.
Unite their hearts as husband and wife,
as they forsake all others.

Living as one in your grace each day,
increasing their love for each other as they walk Your way.
Growing in wisdom and reaching out with Your love.
Jesus, guide them with Your Word and Your love from above.

Casting their cares upon You
and helping each other up when they fall
with You, Lord, as their center,
their forever, All in all.

Eternal God, let them rest in You,
showing Your love to each other in all they say, think, and do.
Faithfully walking through life together in unity,
a picture of Your love for the church now and into eternity.

Amen

Valerie J. Borgal
1996

Therefore a man shall leave his father and mother and be joined to his wife, and they shall become one flesh.

Gen. 2:24
NKJV

Cardinal in Snow

Watercolor
Valerie J. Borgal

An Everlasting Perfect Gift

As God cares for the birds of the fields, much more He cares for us.
Just think about our blessings, and we surely will not fuss.
He gives us breath to breathe and sustains us with food to eat,
not just bread and butter, but some veggies and some meat.
He provided us clothes and shelter from the frigid cold of winter
and made us heal from even a little, tiny splinter.
He gives us family and friends that love us more than we will know,
and talents and abilities to develop as we grow.

God cared for us when He planned for His Son to come long ago.
There was a purpose for this babe as He began to grow;
it was for us He came to earth to clean us as white as snow.
And you may ask how that happened; I guess you would like to know!
Jesus was born to die, shedding His blood for you and me.
He cleanses us through those red drops that spilled from Calvary's tree.
Jesus is the only way to save us from our sin.
We all have broken God's commands, and guilt is dark within.

Jesus is the holy gift. Have you received Him into your heart?
He will forgive and cleanse you and give you a brand new start.
Accept the perfect gift to you that God has given.
It is the gift; there is no other; that lets you into Heaven.
God provided Jesus because we couldn't make it on our own,
He intercedes for you and me as He sits there on His throne.
Along with all nature, let us lift our voices with joy and sing
to the everlasting perfect gift, our gracious heavenly King.

Valerie J.Borgal
2002

Following the Star

Watercolor
Valerie J. Borgal

Camel's Ode to the Creator

Our Masters came to us one day
and said, "We must be on our way!"
With treasures all packed with our gear,
we all stood up and gave a cheer!
They had learned of a star so bright.
It was to be our guiding light.
Everything packed and on our way,
our caravan began to sway.

The reason this star shined so bright,
our Creator was born on that holy night.
Long ago, He spoke and created our universe.
Now He has come to redeem mankind from the curse.
Sin came to all people one horrible day.
In the Garden of Eden, mankind chose to disobey.
But our gracious Creator had a plan
to give His own life and save fallen man.

He came to die for the whole human race
but will rise again, offering His grace.
We are anxious to see Him face to face.
We would like this to be a camel race.
But we must be patient. We will arrive soon.
We will sing Him a happy tune.
We will jump and wiggle and snort with glee
for our Creator, we have come to see.

Valerie J. Borgal

Camel's Ode to the Creator was revised by Rocco DiGloria and he put to music in 2001.
It was written for the Christmas Story Pageant at New England Bible Church, Andover, MA, 2001

When they saw the star, they rejoiced with exceedingly great joy. Matt 2:10 NKJV

Almighty Grace

The new bright star announced His birth
when the Bright Morning Star came to earth.
Light of the world Jesus Christ is He
casting out darkness for all to see.
His word will change the heart,
causing the dread of sin to depart.
From heaven, He came walking the earth,
bringing the promise of the new birth,
teaching goodness, and to be kind.
He gives life to the dead, sight to the blind.
The crowds were amazed, totally awed.
Wonders and miracles proved He is God.
God-man, Messiah, omnipotent One,
the promised Savior, Wonderful Son.
On His head, He bore a thorny crown.
For all our sins, His blood flowed down.
The Son of God went into the grave,
then rose victorious from that cave.
For He is the Way, the Truth, the Life,
washing away sin and ending sin's strife.
The Bread of Life, we feed on His Word;
the scriptures we have eagerly heard.
He saves us by His almighty grace,
offered in love to our lost human race.

Valerie J. Borgal
2007

And the word became flesh and dwelt among
us, and we beheld His glory,
The glory as of the only begotten of the
Father, full of grace and truth.
John 1:14
NKJV

Almighty Grace

Watercolor
Valerie J. Borgal

The Guerard's Chambord

Arriving at the Guerard's Chambord,
I donned my skis and praised the Lord
for a day that dazzled and sparkled with white
against a blue sky so clear and bright.
I crossed over the snow-covered bridge and past the frozen lake.
Into the woods, I skied for a refreshing break.
It was so quiet, peaceful, and, oh, so serene;
what a blessing to take in this snowy white scene.

It brought back to mind a time long ago
when God washed away my sins, making me whiter than snow.
Imagine that, whiter than snow!
How can it be? This is what I know.
Jesus' blood is more powerful than sin.
When I opened my heart to Him and believed it, He came in,
to become my Lord, my Savior, and Friend
and keep me forever after my life here comes to an end.

What about you, my dear friend?
Are you ready for your life to come to an end?
Have you opened the door and believed in your heart?
Has Jesus, the Savior, given you a new start?
He will come to you, He's waiting patiently,
for you to receive forgiveness, to repent, and with Him agree.
He loves you so much; He died in your place;
so you could be whiter than snow, saved by His grace.

Out from the woods, I move a bit slow.
My time out skiing leaves me with an after-glow,
praising my God for helping me to know
the One who makes me whiter than snow.
Crossing over the bridge and onto the pathway
thinking about this glorious day,
and feeling so blessed, I praise my Lord,
while passing by the Guerard's Chambord.

Valerie J. Borgal
1999

Chambord is the name my friends, Paul and Judi, gave their home which
sat on the edge of the conservation land in the town of Andover, MA.

Cross Country Skiing

Watercolor
Valerie J. Borgal

Purge me with hyssop, and I shall be clean; Wash me, and I shall be whiter than snow.

Psalm 51:7
NKJV

Holy Spirit moves
Over the darkened waters
Creator God speaks

Hovering Holy Spirit

Watercolor
Poem and Art
Valerie J Borgal

The earth was without form, and void; and darkness was on the face of the deep.
And the Spirit of God was hovering, over the face of the waters.
Gen. 1:2
NKJV

Holly in Snow

Wax-resist/Watercolor
Valerie J. Borgal

Holly Berries Red

Holly berries red and leaves evergreen
help us to understand the unseen
mysterious plan of our Creator God
when He sent Jesus to become our Lord.

Born as a babe in a lowly manger,
He grew and walked the earth, to men a stranger.
He did many miracles to prove His claim.
He is the Almighty God, the Great I Am!

God's plan played out over the next few years;
for mankind, Jesus shed many tears.
His ultimate sacrifice He made on the cross.
Red like holly berries, His blood cleanses sin's dross.

He makes us whiter than snow when in Him we believe,
like the evergreen leaves, everlasting life we receive.
Let His Spirit guide you, taking away all fear.
May God bless you now and throughout the New Year.

Valerie J. Borgal
2006

in whom we have redemption through His blood, the forgiveness of sins.
Col. 1:14
NKJV

Jewels of Winter

Watercolor
Valerie J. Borgal

For He says to the snow, 'Fall on the earth'; Likewise to the gentle rain and the heavy rain of His strength.

Job 37:6 NKJV

Whiter Than Snow

We woke up to a world of white a few inches deep.
Dressed and went out into the quiet, not even a peep.
No squirrels for Frosty to chase that day,
but lots of snow for us to clear away.

Frosty was wearing no boots, only a sweater.
With snowballs growing on his legs, it didn't seem to matter.
He would stick his nose down under the snow
while mom shoveled instead of having to mow.

With the mower in hibernation, no green grass in sight,
God had painted our world, and His color was white.
Just as He wants to make each person's heart,
changed from the blackness of sin and a new life impart.

He sent His Son to pay for our sins
on the old rugged cross, He wins.
But we need to open the door of our heart,
believing Jesus will enter in and do His part.

Washing away all sin, making us whiter than snow,
so like Jesus, the Savior, we can grow;
born anew from the Spirit with life from above,
now full of peace and awe with the wonder of God's love.

As we look out over the snow so clean and bright,
we thank God for sending His blessed Light.
He cleans away darkness by washing away sin,
giving us salvation; God's wondrous blessin'!

Valerie J. Borgal
1999

My Vain Imagination

Lord, You have given me talents and abilities:
I am learning and growing in my creativity.
You want me to go beyond the now that I know,
meeting each challenge from You and continue to grow.

You remind me that, in You, I can do all things,
but my faith in You sometimes takes wings.
It leaves me with my fanciful imaginations,
reminding me of my frail limitations.

Fear comes and squelches the risk that I must take.
I back off in weakness, Your Presence forsake.
With my eyes off of You I have no wisdom,
no direction, no leading, and no guiding plumb.

My only real hindrance is my imagination;
I forget to trust You and fall into temptation.
Left to myself, I want to hide;
to dwell on the negative and be alone inside.

Your Presence can't shine through me; my light dies,
retreating inward believing Satan's lies.
"It's impossible!" I hear the voice in my ears.
"Your God does not care about you nor understands your fears."

Oh, Lord, my vain imagination has grown so tall.
My pride has run away with me; my faith is so small.
I am not alone, nor is my testing unique;
I should not allow Satan, my soul, to critique.

VBorgal

I must stop, repent, and obey You this hour.
Your forgiveness claim; fill me with Your power.
Mold me as I submit and obey.
Let my imagination soar on Your creative wings today.

I want to live in Your power: in Your love rest;
putting my imagination under the Spirit's control is best.
As others see me trusting in You,
they will glorify You in all I do.

Convict me when I start imagining the absurd.
Keep my heart and mind agreeing with Your Word,
that I am your child, loved and adored,
saved for eternity by You, my precious Lord.

Valerie Borgal
2000

"Casting down imaginations, and every high thing that exalts itself against the knowledge of God,
and bringing into captivity every thought to the obedience of Christ."

2 Cor. 10:5
NKJV

Imagination

Watercolor
Valerie J. Borgal

PAIN

P ain, growing spreading,
A gonizing, excruciating,
I ncreasing, stabbing,
N ever ending, debilitating.

P ain won't allow comfort to come,
A lways making its sordid self known.
I rritating jabs shooting through my body,
N ot giving up, causing me to groan.

P ain is nothing new to You, Jesus.
A t the cross of Calvary, You bore my pain.
I n obedience You took my shame,
N ot wanting me to die in sin's reign.

P ain was excruciating for You, too,
A s You became sin for me.
I n all of the pain You endured,
N eeding to bear my punishment for me to be free.

P ain is something You have experienced.
A lmighty God, You had no light affliction:
I n whippings, beatings, nails, and humiliation.
N ow in my pain comes the Holy Spirit's conviction.

P lease, Lord, in my time of suffering in my sin
A sking for Your forgiveness, You make me clean.
I ncrease my faith as Your Spirit moves in my life.
N o one but You can help me from this pain so mean.

P lease, God, help me endure and be faithful
A ll this suffering that lasts for a moment,
I n comparison to life with You in eternity,
N ever-ending peace and no lament!

P ut your healing touch upon my body.
A gainst the enemy I stand in Your power.
I n the armor of God I dress,
H olding onto Your truth in my final hour.

P utting my trust, in You, my Savior,
A nd taking Your hand, I enter through heaven's door.
I n Your presence, I stand forever,
N ever to experience sin's pain anymore!

G od, you are my Jehovah Raphah, my Healer.
O nly in You do I have a pain-free heavenly home.
N ow in Your presence I'm free at last,
E ternal life with You, my Eternal Shalom!

Valerie Borgal

While experiencing back pain February 29, 2000; I wrote this poem. I dedicate it to my dear friend and merciful sister in the Lord, Eve Lane, who experienced much pain in her battle with cancer. She is now with the Lord, in His presence, pain free, and experiencing heaven, which we, who are living, hope for: trusting in the promises of our faithful God and Savior.

> For we who are in this tent groan, being burdened, not because we want to be unclothed,
> but further clothed, that mortality may be swallowed up by life.

2 Cor. 5:4
NKJV

> Therefore I take pleasure in infirmities, in reproaches, in needs, in persecutions, in distresses,
> for Christ's sake. For when I am weak, then I am strong.

2 Cor. 12:10
NKJV

Crucified for Me

Watercolor
Valerie J. Borgal

The Truest Friend

There is a friend I have I want to tell you about;
He will be the best friend you will ever tout.
This friend's name is Jesus, and He gave up His life;
on the cross of Calvary, He made the supreme sacrifice.

The test of a true friend: greater love has no other,
than to lay down his life for his brother.
And although He died, His life didn't end.
He gives new life to all who believe in Him, my friend!

He's a better friend than I'll ever be,
For He is all-knowing and ever-present, you see.
He knows your troubles; He knows your shame.
He will bring you comfort; so call on His name.

He knows our sin for He paid for each one
on a lonely hill; a victory He won.
He is the Great I AM, the beloved Son,
God in the flesh, the precious Holy One.

He spilled His blood to wash away our sin;
His body was broken for new life to come in.
He loves you with an everlasting love;
you can live with Him in heaven above.

If you will believe and accept Him as Savior,
His Spirit indwells your heart and will help change your behavior.
He will never leave you or forsake you,
not like me; I get busy and absent-minded, too.

So, my friend, in any problem or any situation;
you can have a friend with you who won't go on vacation.
If you receive Jesus, God gives you the power
to become His child in this very hour.

The only way to have sweet peace with God
is to believe in Jesus and make Him your Lord.
Then we will not only be friends, but God's children for eternity,
spending all our future in God's peace and serenity.

Valerie Borgal
2006

In Remembrance

Watercolor
Valerie J. Borgal

For God so loved the world that He gave His only begotten Son,
that whoever believes in Him should not perish but have everlasting life.
For God did not send His Son into the world to condemn the world,
but that the world through Him might be saved.

John 3:16-17
NKJV

and when He had given thanks, He broke it and said, "Take, eat; this is My body which is broken for
you; do this in remembrance of Me." In the same manner He also took the cup after supper, saying,
"This cup is the new covenant in My blood. This do, as often as you drink it in remembrance of Me."
For as often as you eat this bread and drink this cup, you proclaim the Lord's death till He comes.

1Cor. 11:24- 26
NKJV

No Final Goodbye

The day is coming when our life here will end.
We will pass over into eternity given by Jesus, our friend.
We know there is more to come because of our new birth,
but for now, we must use these few moments left here on earth.
New life in Christ we received the day we believed,
and salvation from sin in our life we received.
Life in Jesus, we discovered, brought us peace,
and blessings from Him will always increase.
Each moment we focus on Him as our guide,
He gives wisdom, and opportunities open up wide
to serve Him and use each gift He has given.
Reading His Word has shown us the way to holy livin'.
The Lord had given you the gift of mercy.
You have a heart for others with great sensitivity.
How that gift ministered to me through the years,
as I shared my burdens and shed some tears.
Our bond causes me sorrow as the end draws near,
thinking of losing a friend so dear.
But we both know this is not the end,
it is only a pause from your presence, my friend.
Because one day in the future, we will meet up with each other
and rejoice forever with Jesus, our brother.
In Jesus, we have life forever; we do not die.
Life eternal means no final goodbye.

Valerie J. Borgal
2000

This poem is dedicated to my friend and sister in the Lord, Eve Lane, who spoke into my heart with God's word when I was whining and angry about losing her. She said, in a quiet voice, quoting from the book of Job, "The Lord gives, and the Lord takes away, blessed be the name of the Lord." That shut me up; all I could say was, "Amen." Who am I to argue with the Lord? I stopped my whining and started being grateful and appreciated the time we had together. Because we have trusted Jesus as our Savior, we know, someday, we will see each other again in glory.

We are confident, yes, well pleased rather to be absent from the body and to be present with the Lord.
2 Cor. 5:8
NKJV

Glory

Watercolor
Valerie J. Borgal

But thanks be to God, who gives us the victory through our Lord Jesus Christ.
1Cor. 15:57 NKJV

Poems

Art work

Andrew

Back Cove

Backyard Visitor

Black Sheep

Blueberries

Bryan's Apple

Bugs

Cardinal in the Snow

Cross Country Skiing

Crucified for Me

Fishing in the Rain

Floppy, Green Eared Rabbit?

Following the Star

Frosty

Frosty Catcher

Furry Backyard Clown

Game of Tag

Glory

Holly in Snow

Hovering Holy Spirit

I'd Rather Be a Door Keeper

Imagination

In Remembrance

Jeanne and Frosty

Jewels of Winter

Junco

Leaf Pile

Message in a Bottle

My Palette

O Holy Night

Path to the River

Pemaquid Beauties

Playing in the Cellar on a Hot Summer's Day

Ringing Ears

Skunks

Son Shine

Spices

Spring Awakening

Sweet Friendship

The Cana Cross

The Cottage

The Joker

The Smiling Hat

Will You Still Love Me When I Make A Mess

Printed in the United States
by Baker & Taylor Publisher Services